DINOSAURS

Copyright © 2023 Samuel John

Dinosaurs were creatures that inhabited the Earth millions of years ago.

More specifically, they lived during the **Mesozoic** era, from the **Late Triassic** period to the end of the **Cretaceous**.

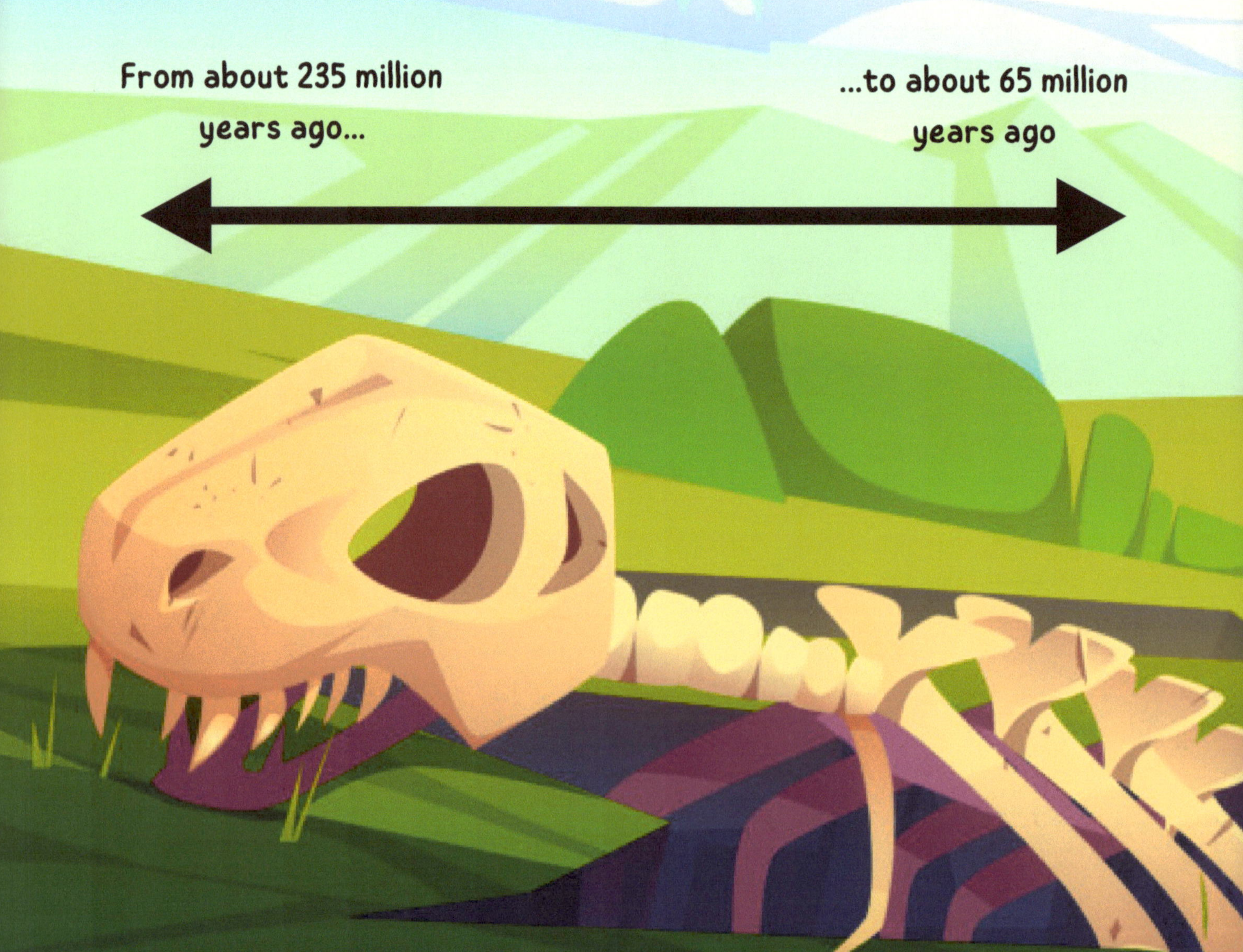

LATE TRIASSIC

It extends from 235 million years ago to roughly 200 million years ago.

JURASSIC

It began 200 million years ago and ended 145 million years ago.

CRETACEOUS

It began 145 million years ago and ended 65 million years ago.

We owe everything we know about dinosaurs to **paleontologists**.

These scientists are devoted to studying the fossils they find.

Fossils: they are remains of petrified bones, teeth, footprints...

WHAT WERE THEY LIKE?

- Dinosaurs were part of the reptile group. They were **vertebrate animals**.
- The majority of the species had their body covered with hard **scales**.
- All were **oviparous**; that is, they hatched from eggs.

- They had four legs and a tail.
- Some of them were massive, like the Brachiosaurus, which could measure 42 ft (13 m) high and 82 ft long (25 m).
- Others were small, like the Compsognathus, which had a maximum length of 5 ft (1.5 m).

WHAT DID THEY EAT?

Dinosaurs could feed on meat, plants, or both.

CARNIVORES

They fed on other animals, such as mammals, fish, insects, and even other dinosaurs.

Tyrannosaurus rex

HERBIVORES

They only ate plants, leaves from trees, and all kinds of vegetation.

Triceratops

OMNIVORES

They could feed on plants, insects, small animals, and even other dinosaurs.

Caudipteryx

WHERE DID THEY LIVE?

One could say that, in general, dinosaurs were land animals.

Some were **quadrupedal** because they walked with their four legs.

Others were **bipedal** because they walked on their back legs. The front ones, by way of arms, were shorter.

Diplodocus

Velociraptor

There were also massive marine reptiles.

They were basically divided into three types: Ichthyosaurs, Plesiosaurs, and Mosasaurs.

Plesiosaur

And there were also flying reptiles, which were the first vertebrates to develop the ability to fly.

Pteranodon

THE BiG 2 GROUPS

Dinosaurs are usually classified into two large groups based on the shape of their hips.

ORNiTHiSCHiANS

Ornithischian dinosaurs were those with hips shaped similarly to those of birds. They were herbivores and feed on plants or vegetables

Iguanodon

SAURISCHIANS

Saurischian dinosaurs were the ones with lizard-like hips. These could be herbivorous or carnivorous, depending on the species.

Apatosaurus
(herbivorous)

Spinosaurus
(carnivorous)

At the end of the book, you will find fact sheets on the best-known dinosaur species! 

WHY DID THEY BECOME EXTINCT?

Even though the real reason for the extinction of the dinosaurs is still unknown, the most accepted theory is that it was due to **the impact of a meteorite on Earth.**

Scientists discovered the impact of a meteorite in the Yucatan peninsula in Mexico, whose age is 65 million years.

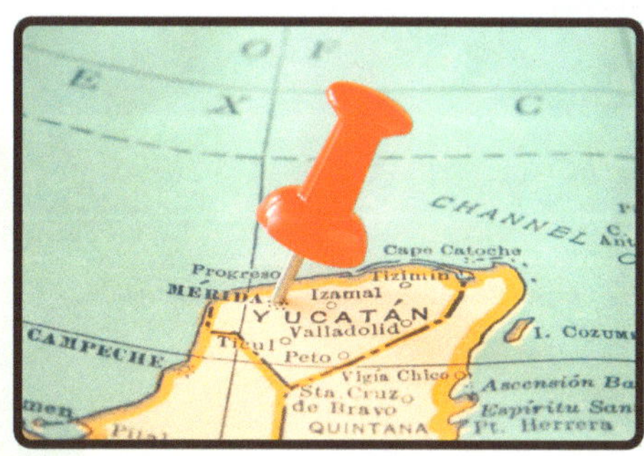

But it wasn't directly the meteorite impact that caused the extinction:

- The impact caused **mega-tsunamis** that swept across almost the entire planet.
- It caused **earthquakes** and **volcanic eruptions**.
- A cloud of **ash** and **dust** blocked out the sunlight. Plants died, and the planet became cold and uninhabitable.

INTERESTING FACTS

There were actually only terrestrial dinosaurs. In fact, note that in the book we have mentioned marine reptiles and flying reptiles, and not marine dinosaurs or flying dinosaurs.

— — — — — —

The word "dinosaur" comes from the Greek deinos (terrible) and saurus (lizard), that is, "terrible lizard".

— — — — — —

Humans did not coexist with dinosaurs. The first humans appeared millions of years after the extinction of the dinosaurs.

Some dinosaurs had tiny arms and large tails to balance their weight so as not to fall forward. This is the case with the T-Rex.

At the time of the dinosaurs, the planet Earth was united into a single continent called Pangea.

It is believed that the first discovery of a dinosaur bone was in China around 3,500 years ago. Nothing was known about dinosaurs yet, so they thought they had discovered a dragon bone.

T- REX

- **Height:** 13 ft (4 meters)
- **Length:** 42.5 ft (13 meters)
- **Weight:** 15,500 lb (7,000 kilograms)
- **Locomotion:** biped
- **Speed:** 19 mph (30 km/h)
- **Group:** Saurischians
- **Diet:** carnivore
- **Period:** Late Cretaceous
- **Name meaning:** the king of the tyrant lizards

- Fossil remains of Tyrannosaurus rex have been found in Canada and the United States.
- His name comes from the Greek word Tyranno and refers to the abuse of his power and superiority over others.

VELOCIRAPTOR

- **Height**: 1.7 ft (0.5 meters)
- **Length**: 6.5 ft (2 meters)
- **Weight**: 33 lb (15 kg)
- **Locomotion**: biped
- **Speed**: 25 mph (40 km/h)
- **Group**: Saurischians
- **Diet**: carnivore
- **Period**: Late Cretaceous
- **Name meaning**: fast hunter

- His fossils have been found in Central Asia, in Mongolia.
- The image beside represents the usual idea of a Velociraptor, but the latest studies show that he could have had feathers.

BRACHIOSAURUS

- **Height:** 42,6 ft (13 meters)
- **Length:** 82 ft (25 meters)
- **Weight:** 31.2 and 51.7 tons (28.3 to 46.9 metric tons)
- **Locomotion:** quadruped
- **Speed:** 12.5 mph (20 km/h)
- **Group:** ornithischians
- **Diet:** herbivore
- **Period:** Late Jurassic
- **Name meaning:** lizard with arms

- His fossils have been found mainly in North America, but they also have been found in Portugal, Algeria, and Tanzania.

- His neck could measure about 29 ft (9 m), which allowed him to feed on the leaves of the tallest trees.

TRICERATOPS

- **Height:** 10 ft (3 meters)
- **Length:** 30 ft (9 meters)
- **Weight:** 5.5–9.9 tons (5–9 metric tons)
- **Locomotion:** quadruped
- **Speed:** 18.5 mph (30 km/h)
- **Group:** ornithischians
- **Diet:** herbivore
- **Period:** Cretaceous
- **Name meaning:** face with three horns

- Triceratops lived in what is now North America.
- Despite his size and ferocious appearance, Triceratops is the most docile and tame dinosaur known.
- His look reminds the current rhinoceros.

DIPLODOCUS

- **Height:** 13 ft (4 meters)
- **Length:** 88.5 ft (27 meters)
- **Weight:** 11 and 17.6 tons (10 to 16 metric tons)
- **Locomotion:** quadruped
- **Speed:** 15 mph (24 km/h)
- **Group:** Saurischians
- **Diet:** herbivore
- **Period:** Late Jurassic
- **Name meaning:** double beam

- His name stems from the double bones in his tail.
- His fossil remains have been discovered in the United States.
- Diplodocus could whip his tail at a speed of over 62 mph (100 km/h)!

STEGOSAURUS

- **Height:** 13 ft (4 meters)
- **Length:** 30 ft (9 meters)
- **Weight:** 4.2 short tons (3.5 metric tons)
- **Locomotion:** biped
- **Speed:** 4.5 mph (7 km/h)
- **Group:** ornithischians
- **Diet:** herbivore
- **Period:** Late Jurassic
- **Name meaning:** roof-lizard

- His name comes from the fact that, at first, it was believed that his plates were laying flat, like tiles on a roof, serving as protection.
- Fossils have been found in North America and Europe.

IGUANODON

- **Height:** 10 ft (3 meters)
- **Length:** 33 ft (10 meters)
- **Weight:** 3.5 tons (3.2 metric tons)
- **Locomotion:** biped/quadruped
- **Speed:** 15 mph (24 km/h)
- **Group:** ornithischians
- **Diet:** herbivore
- **Period:** Early Cretaceous
- **Name meaning:** iguana-tooth

- His name comes from the resemblance of his teeth to those of today's iguanas.
- Iguanodon fossils have been found in different places: Spain, Belgium, England, Germany, the United States, and North Africa.

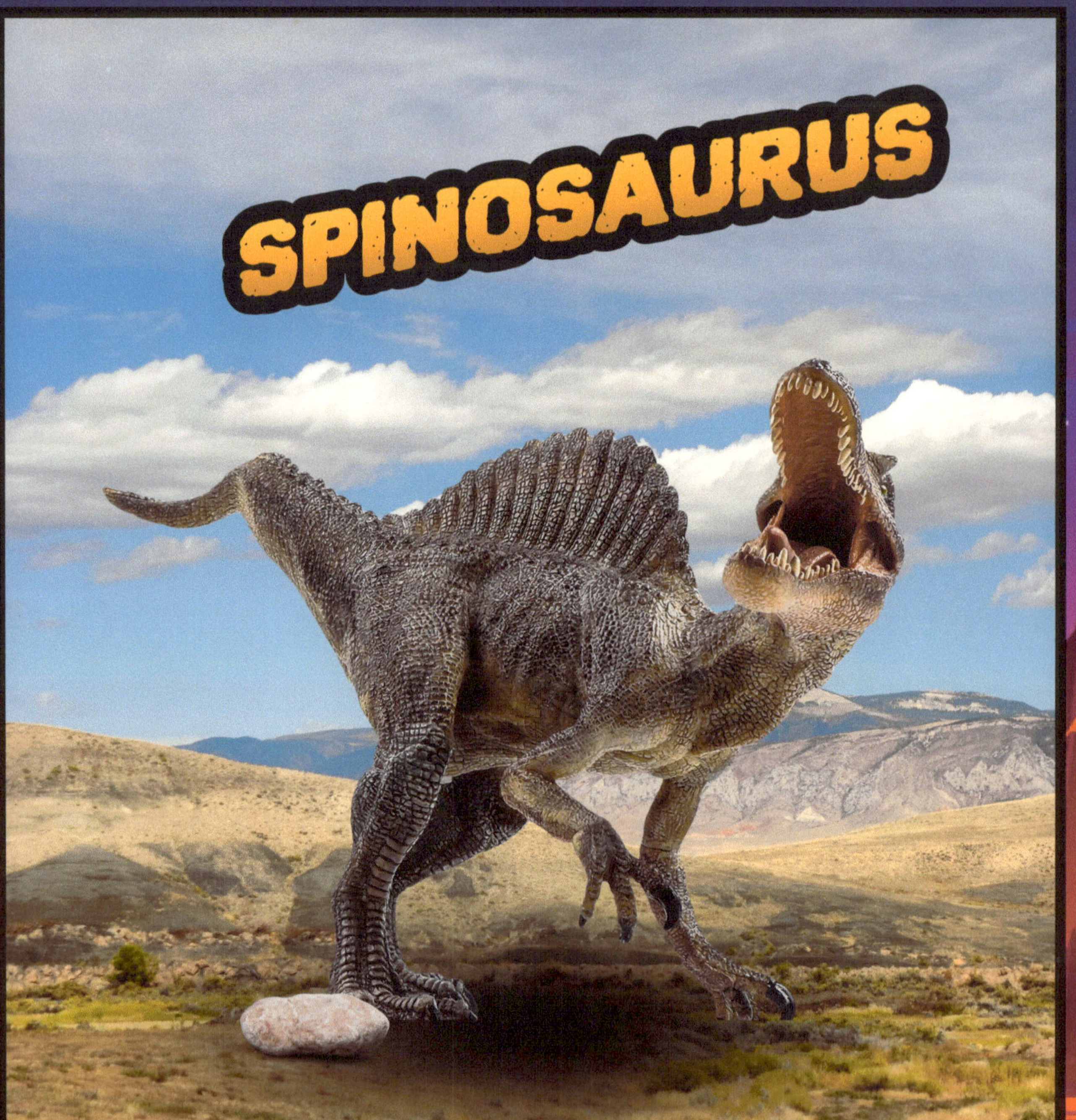
SPINOSAURUS

- **Height:** 16.5 ft (5 meters)
- **Length:** 50 ft (15 meters)
- **Weight:** 7.7 to 9.9 tons (7 to 9 metric tons)
- **Locomotion:** biped
- **Speed:** 9 mph (14.5 km/h)
- **Group:** Saurischians
- **Diet:** carnivore
- **Period:** Cretaceous
- **Meaning name:** spine lizard

- The name refers to its large dorsal fin.
- It was probably the largest carnivorous dinosaur, surpassing even the feared T-Rex!
- He could move at great speed through the water, where he hunted his prey.

PARASAUROLOPHUS

- **Height:** 13 ft (4 meters)
- **Length:** 32 ft (10 meters)
- **Weight:** 4.4 short tons (4 metric tons)
- **Locomotion:** biped/quadruped
- **Speed:** 22 mph 35.5 km/h
- **Group:** ornithischians
- **Diet:** herbivore
- **Period:** Late Cretaceous
- **Name meaning:** near crested lizard

- His name is due to its resemblance to the Saurolophus ("crested lizard").
- His fossils have been found in areas of Canada and the United States.

ANKYLOSAURUS

- **Height:** 6.5 ft (2 meters)
- **Length:** 26 ft (8 meters)
- **Weight:** 6.5 short tons (5.9 metric tons)
- **Locomotion:** quadruped
- **Speed:** 12.5 mph (20 km/h)
- **Group:** ornithischians
- **Diet:** herbivore
- **Period:** Late Cretaceous
- **Name meaning:** fused lizard

- He had armor made up of bony plates that covered his entire body, apart from his belly.
- His tail finished in the shape of a hammer-like is also characteristic.
- He lived in the area of what is now North America.

MAMENCHISAURUS

- **Height:** 33 ft (10 meters)
- **Length:** 82 ft (25 meters)
- **Weight:** 16.5 tons (15 metric tons)
- **Locomotion:** biped
- **Speed:** 8 mph (13 km/h)
- **Group:** Saurischians
- **Diet:** herbivore
- **Period:** Late Jurassic
- **Name meaning:** Mamenchi lizard

- His fossil remains have been found in China.
- His neck stands out, which could measure almost half of his entire body, about 32 ft (10 meters).

DILOPHOSAURUS

- **Height**: 6.5 ft (2 meters)
- **Length**: 23 ft (7 meters)
- **Weight**: 880 lb (400 kg)
- **Locomotion**: biped
- **Speed**: 25 mph (40 km/h)
- **Group**: Saurischians
- **Diet**: carnivore
- **Period**: Early Jurassic
- **Name meaning**: two-crested lizard

- Dilophosaurus lived in what is now North America.
- It's known for the scene in the movie "Jurassic Park" in which he spits poison. The truth is that he could not spit acid or venom. He also did not have a deployable membrane around his neck, as also shown in the movie.

We have reached the end.

Undoubtedly, the world of dinosaurs is full of surprising things.

Every year new things are learned about them, and even new species are discovered. It will be very interesting to know what new data we will obtain, from now on, on these fantastic beings that inhabited our planet millions of years before our existence.

I hope you liked it and that you learned new things.

I want to ask you a favor so that this book reaches more people, and that is that you rate it with a sincere opinion on the platform where you purchased it.

With that small gesture, you will be helping me to carry on with new projects.

I can't wait to start creating
my next book for you!

See you soon!

KEEP LEARNING...

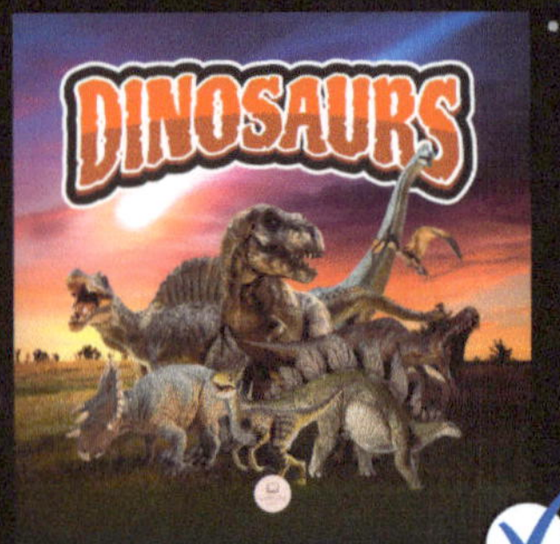

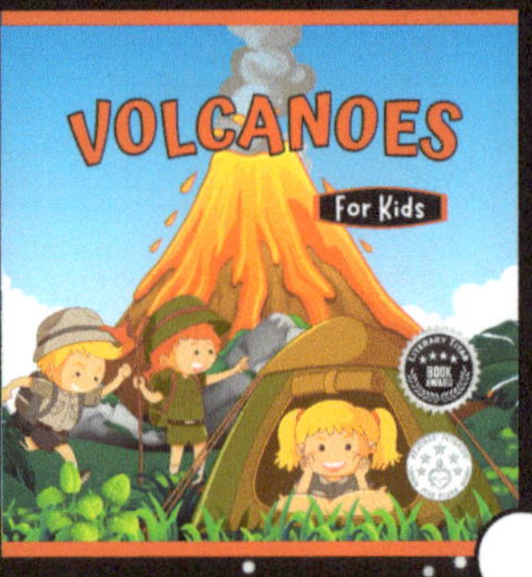

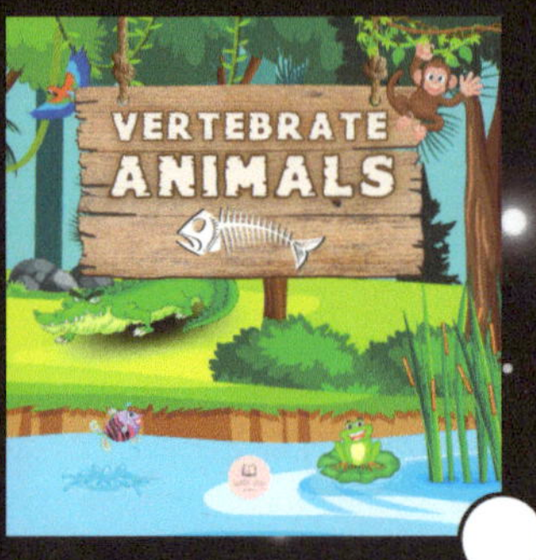

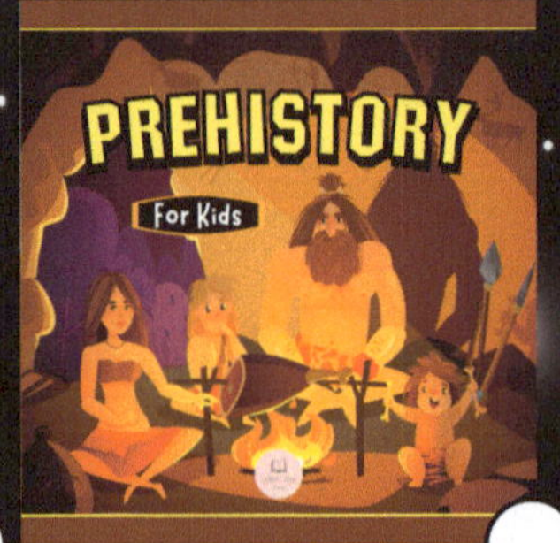

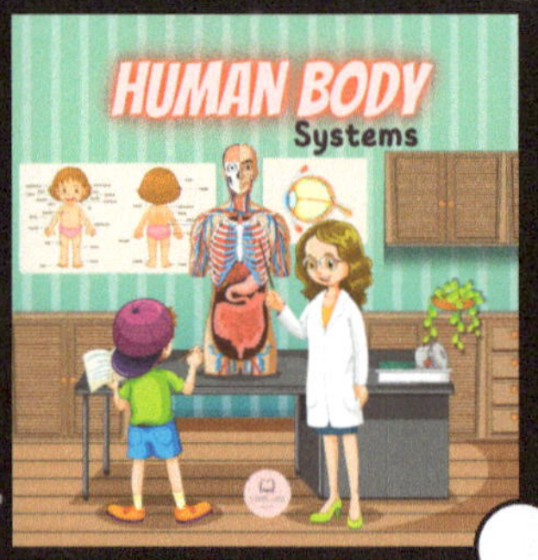

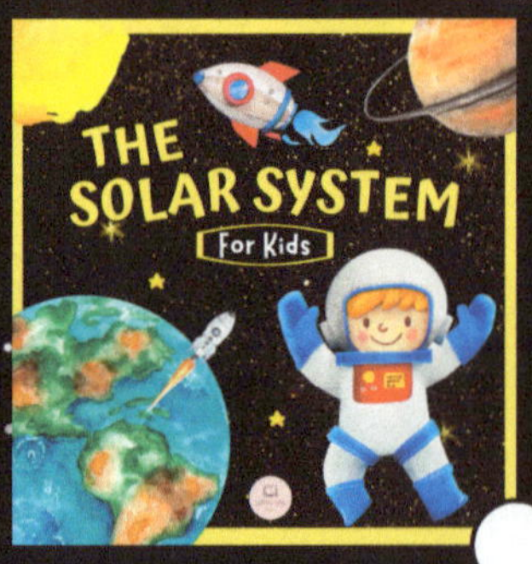

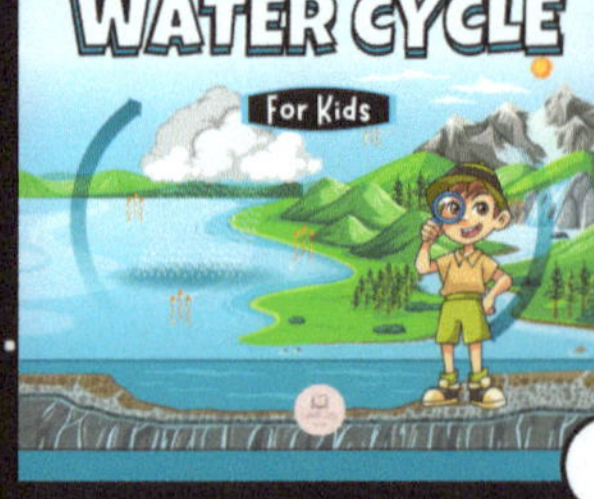

https://www.pge.me/childrensbooks